THE

# CIVIL WAR

## HANDBOOK

by William H. Price

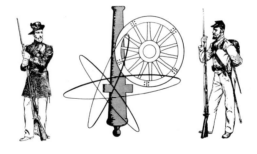

Published by
L.B. Prince Co., Inc.
6621-C Electronic Drive
Springfield, Va 22151

Copyright 1961
Printed in U.S.A.

ISBN# 1-879295-00-8

Cover by Jack Woodson

# THE CIVIL WAR

*Here brothers fought for their principles*
*Here heroes died to save their country*
*And a united people will forever cherish*
*the precious legacy of their noble manhood.*

*—PENNSYLVANIA MONUMENT AT VICKSBURG*

The Civil War, which began in the 1830's as a cold war and moved toward the inevitable conflict somewhere between 1850 and 1860, was one of America's greatest emotional experiences. When the war finally broke in 1861, beliefs and political ideals had become so firm that they transcended family ties and bonds of friendship — brother was cast against brother. The story of this supreme test of our Nation, though one of tragedy, is also one of triumph, for it united a nation that had been divided for over a quarter century.

Holding a place in history midway between the Revolutionary War of the 18th century and the First World War of the 20th, the American Civil War had far-reaching effects: by the many innovations and developments it stimulated, it became the forerunner of modern warfare; by the demands it made on technology and production, it hastened the industrial revolution in America. This conflict also provided the ferment from which great personalities arise. Qualities of true greatness were revealed in men like William Tecumseh Sherman, the most brilliant strategist of modern times; Nathan Bedford Forrest, one of the greatest of natural born leaders; Robert E. Lee, "one of the supremely gifted men produced by our Nation"; and Abraham Lincoln, who, like the other great men of that era, would be minor characters in our history had they not been called upon in this time of crisis. And emerging from such trying times were seven future Presidents of the United States, all officers of the Union Army.

But the story of this sectional struggle is not only one of great leaders and events. It is the story of 18,000 men in Gen. Sedgwick's Corps who formed a marching column that stretched over ten miles of road, and in that hot month of July 1863, the story of how they marched steadily for eighteen hours, stopping only once to rest, until they reached Gettysburg where the crucial battle was raging. It is the story of more than two hundred young VMI Cadets, who without hesitation left their classrooms to fight alongside hardened veterans at the battle of New Market in 1864. Or it is the story of two brothers who followed different flags and then met under such tragic circumstances on the field of battle at Petersburg.

It is also a story of the human toil and machinery that produced more than four million small arms for the Union Army and stamped from copper over one billion percussion caps for these weapons during the four years of war. Inside the Confederacy, it is the story of experiments with new weapons -- the submarine, iron-clad rams, torpedoes, and landmines -- in an attempt to overcome the North's numerical superiority.

It is the purpose of *The Civil War Handbook* to present this unusual story of the Civil Warm a mosaic composed of fragments from the lesser-known and yet colorful facts that have survived a century but have been obscured by the voluminous battle narratives and campaign studies.

Much of this material, when originally drafted, was selected by the National Civil War Centennial Commission for their informative and interesting *Facts About the Civil War.* This original material, revised and enlarged, has grown into *The Civil War Handbook.*

The handbook is divided into five basic parts. The first is a presentation of little-known and unusual facts about participants, battles and losses, and the cost of war. The second is a graphic portrayal of both the men and machines that made the war of the 1860's. The special selection of photographs for this portion of the story were made available through the courtesy of the National Archives and the Library of Congress. Next are reproductions in color of Union and Confederate uniforms from the *Official Records Atlas* and the famous paintings by H. A. Ogden. The fourth section is a reference table of battles and losses listed in chronological order, accompanied by a map showing the major engagements of the war. And primarily for the growing number of new Civil War buffs, there is a roster of Civil War Round Tables, as well as a recommended list of outstanding books on the Civil War.

The material presented in *The Civil War Handbook* has been selected from standard sources, the most outstanding of which are: the *Official Records of the Union and Confederate Armies and Navies*, Moore's *Rebellion Record*, Cullum's *Biographical Register of West Point Graduates*, Phisterer's *Statistical Record*, Livermore's *Numbers and Losses in the Civil War*, Fox's *Regimental Losses*, the *Dictionary of American Biography*, Dyer's *Compendium of the War of the Rebellion*, the *Annual Reports of the Secretary of War*, and last but far from least, one of the richest sources of information available, my fellow members of the District of Columbia Civil War Round Table.

# THE FIRST MODERN WAR

*In the arts of life, man invents nothing; but in the arts
of death he outdoes Nature herself, and produces by
chemistry and machinery all the slaughter of plague,
pestilence and famine.*
                    *— GEORGE BERNARD SHAW*

The arts of tactics and strategy were revolutionized by the many
developments introduced during the 1860's. Thus the Civil War
ushered in a new era in warfare with the . . .

FIRST practical machine gun.
FIRST repeating rifle used in combat.
FIRST use of the railroads as a major means of transporting troops and supplies.
FIRST mobile siege artillery mounted on rail cars.
FIRST extensive use of trenches and field fortifications.
FIRST large-scale use of land mines, known as "subterranean shells".
FIRST naval mines or "torpedoes".
FIRST ironclad ships engaged in combat.
FIRST multi-manned submarine.
FIRST organized and systematic care of the wounded on the battlefield.
FIRST widespread use of rails for hospital trains.
FIRST organized military signal service.
FIRST visual signaling by flag and torch during combat.
FIRST use of portable telegraph units on the battlefield.
FIRST military reconnaissance from a manned balloon.
FIRST draft in the United States.
FIRST organized use of Negro troops in combat.
FIRST voting in the field for a national election by servicemen.
FIRST income tax — levied to finance the war.
FIRST photograph taken in combat.
FIRST Medal of Honor awarded an American soldier.

# Brother Against Brother

*"And why should we not accord them equal honor, for they were both Americans, imbued with those qualities which have made this country great."*

— BELL IRVIN WILEY

PRESIDENT LINCOLN, the Commander-In-Chief of the Union Army, had four brothers-in-law in the Confederate Army, and three of his sisters-in-law were married to Confederate officers.

JEFFERSON DAVIS, Commander-in-Chief of the Confederate Army, served the U.S. Army as a colonel during the Mexican War and held the post of Secretary of War in President Pierce's cabinet. Previously, as a senior United States Senator, he had been Chairman of the Senate Military Affairs Committee. Lincoln and Davis were born in Kentucky, the only state that has ever had two of its sons serve as President at the same time.

JOHN TYLER, 10th President of the United States, was elected to the Confederate States Congress in 1862, but died before it convened. On March 4, 1861, Tyler's granddaughter unfurled the first flag of the Confederacy when it was raised over the Confederate Capitol at Montgomery, Alabama.

The Battle of Lynchburg, Virginia, in June 1864 brought together two future Presidents of the United States — General RUTHERFORD B. HAYES and Major WILLIAM McKINLEY, U.S.A. — and a former Vice-President -- General JOHN C. BRECKINRIDGE, C.S.A. Five other Union generals later rose to the Presidency: ANDREW JOHNSON, U.S. GRANT, JAMES A. GARFIELD, CHESTER A. ARTHUR, and BENJAMIN HARRISON.

The four Secretaries of War during the eleven years prior to the Civil War were all from the South. All four later held office in the Confederate government.

Fourteen of the 26 Confederate Senators had previously served in the United States Congress. In the Confederate House of Representatives, 33 members were former U.S. Congressmen.

Confederate Generals ROBERT E. LEE and P.G.T. BEAUREGARD both ranked second in their graduating classes at West Point, and both officers later returned to hold the position of Superintendent of the Academy. Lee's appointment to the rank of full colonel in the United States Army was signed by President Lincoln.

In 1859 WILLIAM TECUMSEH SHERMAN was appointed the first president of what is today the Louisiana State University. Although his chief claim to fame was the destructive "March to the Sea", a portrait of the Union general occupies a prominent place in the Memorial Tower of this Southern university.

Over one-fourth of the West Point graduates who fought during the Civil War were in the Confederate Army. Half of the 304 who served in Gray were on active duty in the United States Army when war broke out. Of the total number of West Pointers who went South, 148 were promoted to the rank of general officer. In all, 313 of the 1,098 officers in the United States Army joined the Confederacy.

One fourth of the officers in the United States Navy resigned to cast their lot with the Confederate Navy. Of the 322 who resigned, 243 were line officers.

When J.E.B. STUART raided Chambersburg, Pennsylvania, in 1862, he was pursued by Federal cavalry under the command of his father-in-law, Brig.Gen. PHILIP ST. GEORGE COOKE, whose name is frequently confused with that of Confederate General PHILIP ST. GEORGE COCKE, both West Pointers. As if that weren't bad enough, there was a Union general by the name of JEFFERSON DAVIS.

WILLIAM T. MAGRUDER (U.S.M.A. 1850) commanded a squadron of the 1st United States Cavalry at First Manassas and during the Peninsula Campaign. In August 1862 he was granted leave of absence, and two months later he switched loyalties to join the Confederate Army. On July 3, 1863, he fell during the famous charge at Gettysburg.

The Virginia Military Institute graduated WILLIAM H. GILLESPIE in the special war class of 1862. While awaiting his appointment as an officer on "Stonewall" Jackson's staff, he deserted to the Union Army and became Adjutant of the 14th West Virginia Cavalry.

If Blue and Gray didn't meet again at Gettysburg during the annual reunions, they at least met on the banks of the Nile. No less than

50 former Union and Confederate officers held the rank of colonel or above in the Army of the Khedive during the 1870's. Two ex-Confederate generals and three former Union officers attained the rank of general in the Egyptian Army, holding such positions as Chief of Staff, Chief of Engineers, and Chief Ordnance Officer.

Only three Confederates ever held the rank of general in the United States Army following the Civil War -- MATTHEW C. BUTLER, FITZHUGH LEE, and JOE WHEELER. Lee and Wheeler, though they served as generals in the Confederate Army as well as in the United States Army during the Spanish American War, both graduated at the bottom of their West Point classes. When Lee and Wheeler were promoted to major general in 1901, their commissions were signed by a former Yankee officer -- President William McKinley.

General GEORGE PICKETT, a native Virginian, was appointed to the United States Military Academy from the State of Illinois. John Todd Stuart obtained the appointment at the request of his law partner, Abraham Lincoln.

The senior general in the Confederate Army, SAMUEL COOPER, hailed from New York. Before the war, he had been Adjutant General of the United States Army. From 1861 to 1865 he was the Adjutant and Inspector General of the Confederate Army.

Fort Sumter was surrendered in 1861 by a Kentucky-born Union officer, Major ROBERT ANDERSON. Confederate General JOHN C. PEMBERTON, a Pennsylvanian by birth, surrendered Vicksburg in 1863. There was no collusion in either surrender; both men were loyal supporters of their respective causes.

The first Superintendent of the United States Naval Academy, Commodore FRANKLIN BUCHANAN, commanded the C.S.S. *Virginia (Merrimac)* in its first engagement. On the first ship to surrender under the *Virginia's* guns was Buchanan's brother, an officer of the U.S. Navy.

Major CLIFTON PRENTISS of the 6th Maryland Infantry (Union) and his younger brother WILLIAM, of the 2nd Maryland Infantry (Confederate), were both mortally wounded when their regiments clashed at Petersburg on April 2, 1865 — just seven days before hostilities ceased. Both were removed from the battlefield and after a separation of four years, they were taken to the same hospital in Washington. Each fought and each died for his cause.

# THEY ALSO SERVED

*Fame is the echo of actions, resounding them to the world, save that the echo repeats only the last part, but fame relates all . . . . .*

*— FULLER*

Poet SIDNEY LANIER fought as a private in the 2nd Georgia Battalion during the Seven Days' Battles near Richmond. In November 1862 he was captured on a Confederate blockade-runner and imprisoned at Point Lookout, Maryland. Sixteen years after the war he died from tuberculosis contracted while in prison.

New England poet ALBERT PIKE commanded the Confederate Department of Indian Territory. He wrote the stanzas of the popular Southern version of *Dixie,* a tune which originated not in the South, but in New York City during the 1850's.

At the battle of the Monocacy in 1864 Union General LEW WALLACE, author of *Ben-Hur,* commanded the force defending Washington against General Jubal Early's attack. After the war he served as Governor of New Mexico and Minister to Turkey.

When the Marion Rangers organized in 1861, SAMUEL CLEMENS (Mark Twain) joined as a lieutenant, but he left this Missouri Company before it was mustered into Confederate service, having fired only one hostile shot during the war.

Confederate Private HENRY MORTON STANLEY, of "Doctor Livingstone, I presume" fame, survived a bloody charge at Shiloh only to be taken prisoner. Later he joined the Union ranks and finished the war in Yankee blue.

ANDREW CARNEGIE was a young man in his mid-twenties when he left his position as superintendent of the Pittsburgh Division, Pennsylvania Railroad to pitch in with workers rebuilding the rail line from Annapolis to Washington. Later in 1861 he was given the position of superintendent of military railways and government telegraph.

HENRY A. DUPONT, grandson of the DuPont industries founder, was awarded the Congressional Medal of Honor for gallantry at the battle of Cedar Creek in October 1864. Captain DuPont, who had graduated from West Point at the head of his class in 1861, went on to serve as United States Senator from Delaware.

ELIAS HOWE presented each field and staff officer of the 5th Massachusetts Regiment with a stallion fully equipped for service. Later, he volunteered as a private, and when the State failed to pay his unit, he met the regimental payroll with his own money.

At the age of 15 GEORGE WESTINGHOUSE ran away from home and joined the Union Army. Neither he nor Elias Howe rose to officer rank, but both are today in the Hall of Fame for their achievements — the air brake and the sewing machine.

In 1861 CORNELIUS VANDERBILT presented a high-speed side-wheel steamer to the United States Navy. At the time, there were less than 50 ships in active naval service. The cruiser, named the *Vanderbilt*, captured three blockade-runners during the war and in 1865 participated in the bombardment and amphibious assault on Fort Fisher. The Federal Navy at that time had grown to a fleet of more than 550 steam-powered ships.

Admiral GEORGE DEWEY, of Manila Bay fame, served as a young lieutenant under Admiral Farragut during the attack on Port Hudson in 1863. His ship was the only one lost in the engagement.

Colonel CHRISTOPHER C. ("Kit") CARSON commanded the 1st New Mexico Volunteers (Union), and campaigned against the Comanche, Navajo, and Apache Indians during the Civil War. In 1866 he was promoted to brigadier general.

In his mid-teens JESSE JAMES joined the Confederate raiders led by William Quantrill. The famous "Dead or alive" reward for Jesse in 1882 was issued by an ex-Confederate officer, Governor Thomas T. Crittenden of Missouri.

# The Soldier, The Battle, The Losses

*"There's many a boy here today who looks on war as all glory, but, boys, it is all hell."*
— *WILLIAM TECUMSEH SHERMAN*

Of the 2.3 million men enlisted in the Union Army, seventy per cent were under 23 years of age. Approximately 100,000 were 16 and an equal number 15. Three hundred lads were 13 or less, and the records show that there were 25 no older than 10 years.

The average infantry regiment of 10 companies consisted of 30 line officers and 1300 men. However, by the time a new regiment reached the battlefield, it would often have less than 800 men available for combat duty. Sickness and details as cooks, teamsters, servants, and clerks accounted for the greatly reduced numbers. Actually, in many of the large battles the regimental fighting strength averaged no more than 480 men.

In 1864 the basic daily ration for a Union soldier was (in ounces): 20—beef, 18—flour, 2.56—dry beans, 1.6—green coffee, 2.4—sugar, .64—salt, and smaller amounts of pepper, yeast powder, soap, candles, and vinegar. While campaigning, soldiers seldom obtained their full ration and many had to forage for subsistence.

In the Army of Northern Virginia in 1863 the rations available for every 100 Confederate soldiers over a 30-day period consisted of 1/4 lb. of bacon, 18 oz. of flour, 10 lbs. of rice, and a small amount of peas and dried fruit—when they could be obtained. (It is little wonder that Lee elected to carry the war into Pennsylvania—if for no other reason than to obtain food for an undernourished army.)

During the Shenandoah Valley campaign of 1862 "Stonewall" Jackson marched his force of 16,000 men more than 600 miles in 35 days. Five major battles were fought and four separate Union armies, totaling 63,000, were defeated.

In June 1864, the U.S.S. *Kearsarge* sank the C.S.S. *Alabama* in a fierce engagement in the English Channel off Cherbourg, France. Frenchmen gathered along the beach to witness the hour-long duel, which inspired a young French artist, Edouard Manet, to paint the battle scene that now hangs in the Philadelphia Museum of Art.

The Confederate cruiser *Shenandoah* sailed completely around the world raiding Union commerce vessels and whalers. The ship and crew surrendered to British authorities at Liverpool in November 1865, seven months after Lee's surrender at Appomattox.

The greatest naval bombardment during the war was on Christmas Eve, 1864, at Fort Fisher, North Carolina. Fifty-seven vessels, with a total of 670 guns, were engaged—the largest fleet ever assembled by the U.S. Navy up to that time. The Army, Navy, and Marines combined in a joint operation to reduce and capture the fort.

In July, 1862 the first Negro troops of the Civil War were organized by General David Hunter. Known as the 1st South Carolina Regiment, they were later designated the 33rd Regiment United States Colored Troops. Some 186,000 Negro soldiers served in the Union Army, 4,300 of whom became battle casualties.

At the battle of Fredericksburg in 1862, the line of Confederate trenches extended a distance of seven miles. The troop density in these defensive works was 11,000 per mile.

Over 900 guns and mortars bristled from the 68 forts defending the Nation's Capital during the war. The fortifications, constructed by the Engineer Corps during the early part of the war, circled the city on a 37-mile perimeter.

During Sherman's campaign from Chattanooga to Atlanta, the Union Army of the Tennessee, in a period of four months, constructed over 300 miles of rifle pits, fired 149,670 artillery rounds and 22,137,132 rounds of small-arms ammunition.

To fire a Civil War musket, eleven separate motions had to be made. The regulation in the 1860's specified that a soldier should fire three aimed shots per minute, allowing 20 seconds per shot and less than two seconds per motion.

At the battle of Stone's River, Tennessee, in January, 1863, the Federal infantry in three days exhausted over 2,000,000 rounds of ammunition, and the artillery fired 20,307 rounds. The total weight of the projectiles was in excess of 375,000 pounds.

At the Battle of First Bull Run or Manassas, it has been estimated that between 8,000 and 10,000 bullets were fired for every man killed and wounded.

The campaign against Petersburg, the longest sustained operation of the war, began in the summer of 1864 and lasted for 10 months, until the spring of '65. The fighting covered an area of more than 170 square miles, with 35 miles of trenches and fortifications stretching from Richmond to the southwest of Petersburg. During September, 1864, nearly 175 field and siege guns poured forth a daily average of 7.8 tons of iron on the Confederate works.

The greatest cavalry battle in the history of the western hemisphere was fought at Brandy Station, Virginia, on June 9, 1863. Nearly 20,000 cavalrymen were engaged for more than 12 hours. At the height of the battle, along Fleetwood Hill, charges and countercharges were made continuously for almost three hours.

The greatest regimental loss of the entire war was borne by the 1st Maine Heavy Artillery. The unit saw no action until 1864, but in the short span of less than one year, over half of its 2,202 men engaged in battle were hit. In the assault on Petersburg in June, 1864, the regiment lost 604 men killed and wounded in less than 20 minutes.

The largest regimental loss in a single battle was suffered by the 26th North Carolina Infantry at Gettysburg. The regiment went into battle with a little over 800 men, and by the end of the third day, 708 were dead, wounded, or missing. In one company of 84, every officer and man was hit.

Of the 46 Confederate regiments that went into the famous charge at Gettysburg on July 3, 1863, 15 were commanded by General Pickett. Thirteen of his regiments were led by Virginia Military Institute graduates; only two of them survived the charge.

The heaviest numerical loss during any single battle was at Gettysburg, where 40,322 Americans were killed or wounded. On the Union side 21 per cent of those engaged were killed or wounded, in the Confederate ranks 30 per cent—the largest percentage of Confederates hit in any battle. The largest percentage of Union soldiers hit in battle was at Port Hudson in May 1863, where 26.7 per cent of those engaged were killed or wounded.

During May and June 1864 the Armies of the Potomac and the James lost 77,452 men—a greater number than Lee had in his entire army.

Union Army hospitals treated over 6 million cases during the war. There were twice as many deaths from disease as from hostile bullets. Diarrhea and dysentery alone took the lives of 44,558 Union soldiers.

From 1861-1865 the Quartermaster Corps of the Union Army made 116,148 burials.

In the 79 National Civil War cemeteries, 54 per cent of the graves are those of unknown soldiers. The largest Civil War cemetery is at Vicksburg, where 16,000 soldiers rest; only 3,896 are known. At the Confederate prison site in Salisbury, North Carolina, where 12,126 Union soldiers are buried, 99 per cent are unknown.

# THE COST OF WAR

*Nor deem the irrevocable Past*
*As wholly wasted, wholly vain,*
*If, rising on its wrecks, at last*
*To something nobler we attain.*
— *HENRY WADSWORTH LONGFELLOW*

From 1861 — 1865 it cost the United States Government approximately 2 million dollars a day to prosecute the war; the Second World War cost more than 113 million dollars a day.

In 1880 the Secretary of the Treasury reported that the Civil War had cost the Federal Government 6.19 billion dollars. By 1910 the cost of the war, including pensions and other veterans benefits, had reached 11.5 billion dollars. World War II was three months shorter than the Civil War, but from 1942-1945 approximately 156 billion dollars was spent on the military establishment.

The total cost of the war to the South has been estimated at 4 billion dollars.

The public debt outstanding for an average population of 33 million rose from $2.80 to $75 per capita between 1861 and 1865. In mid-1958 the per capita debt stood at $1,493 for a population of 175.5 million.

In 1958 the government was providing pensions for 3,042 widows of Union veterans. In June of that year, as a result of special legislation, 526 widows of Southern soldiers and the two surviving Confederate veterans became eligible for Federal pensions. The last Union veteran, Albert Woolson, had died in 1956, leaving the two Confederates, John Salling and Walter Williams, to draw the highest Civil War pensions paid by the United States Government. The last Civil War veteran, Walter Williams, died in December 1959 at the age of 117. Since then, William's claim as a veteran has been disputed in the newspapers, but sufficient evidence does not exist to positively prove or disprove his military status.

The pursuit and capture of Jefferson Davis at Irwinville, Georgia, cost the Federal Government $97,031.62.

From 1861 — 1865 it cost the Federal government, in millions of dollars:

$727 - to clothe and feed the Army
  18 - to clothe and feed the Navy
 339 - for transportation of troops and supplies
 127 - for cavalry and artillery horses
  76 - for the purchase of arms
   8 - to maintain and provide for Confederate prisoners

Soldiers and sailors of the United States received 1.34 billion dollars in pay during the war.

In 1861 an infantry private was paid $13 per month—compared to a private's pay of $83 today. A Civil War colonel drew $95 per month and a brigadier general $124. Their counterparts today are paid a monthly base rate of $592 and $800.

During the 1860's the average cost of a musket was $13 as compared to $105 for an M1 Garand in World War II.

# NUMBERS AND LOSSES

| | North | South [1] |
|---|---|---|
| Population | 22,400,000 | 9,103,000 [2] |
| Military Age Group (18-45) | 4,600,000 | 985,000 |
| Trained Militia 1827-1861 | 2,470,000 | 692,000 |
| Regular Army January, 1861 | 16,400 | 0 |
| Military Potential 1861 | 2,486,400 | 692,000 |
| Total Individuals in Service 1861-1865 | 2,213,400 | 1,003,600 |
| | | |
| Total Strength July, 1861 | 219,400 | 114,000 |
| Total Strength January, 1863 | 962,300 | 450,200 |
| Peak Strength 1864-1865 | 1,044,660 | 484,800 |
| Army | 980,100 | 481,200 |
| Navy | 60,700 | 3,000 |
| Marines | 3,860 | 600 |
| | | |
| Total Hit in Battle | 385,100 | 320,000 |
| Total Battle Deaths | 110,100 | 94,000 |
| Killed in Battle | 67,100 | 54,000 |
| Died of Wounds | 43,000 | 40,000 |
| Wounded (not mortally) [3] | 275,000 | 226,000 |
| Missing in Action | 6,750 | --- |
| Captured [4] | 211,400 | 462,000 |
| Died in Prison | 30,200 | 26,000 |
| Died of Disease | 224,000 | 60,000 |
| Other Deaths | 34,800 | --- |
| Desertions [5] | 199,000 | 83,400 |
| Discharged | 426,500 | 57,800 |
| Surrendered 1865 | | 174,223 |

1. Confederate figures are based upon the best information and estimates available.
2. Includes 3,760,000 slaves in the seceded states.
3. A number of these were returned to duty. In the Union Army, those who were not fit for combat were placed in the Veteran Reserve Corps and performed administrative duties.
4. An undetermined number were exchanged and returned to duty.
5. Many deserters returned to duty. In the Union Army, where $300 bounty was paid for a 3-year enlistment, it was not uncommon to find a soldier picking up his bounty in one regiment and then deserting to join another unit just for the additional bounty.

ABRAHAM LINCOLN
PRESIDENT
UNITED STATES OF AMERICA

JEFFERSON DAVIS
PRESIDENT
CONFEDERATE STATES OF AMERICA

None too military in appearance, such ragged squads of men and boys developed into an army that marched an average of 16 miles a day.

Smartly dressed amphibious soldiers. Some of the 3,000 U.S. Marines of the Civil War made landings on Southern coasts, but the majority served as gun crews aboard ship.

Jack-tars of the old Navy saw plenty of action in clearing the Mississippi and chasing down Confederate raiders of the high seas. Because of the high bounties and pay, many foreign seafarers were attracted to both navies.

21

*Ill-clad and poorly equipped, Confederate volunteers at Pensacola, Florida, wait their turn for the smell of black powder.*

*On the silent battlefield at Gettysburg, veterans of Lee's Army of Northern Virginia who survived the baptism by fire await their fate as prisoners of war.*

Regimental camp sites created sanitary problems that went unsolved. Typhoid fever, diarrhea, and dysentery took the lives of over 70,000 Union soldiers.

Private residences like the Wallach House at Culpeper, Virginia, provided generals on both sides with comfortable quarters in the field. Staff officers were usually tented on the lawns.

24

Log cabins often replaced tents during the winter months when campaigning slackened and the armies settled down. In some camps it was not uncommon to find visiting army wives.

Soldiers turned to a variety of activities to break the long days and weeks of monotonous camplife. Even officers were not immune to the horseplay.

When two or more Yanks or Rebs gathered together, a deck of cards often made its appearance. Fearful of an angry God, soldiers usually discarded such instruments of sin before entering battle.

*Chess, a favorite pastime in camp, finds Colonel Martin McMahon, General Sedgwick's adjutant, engaged in the contest that was a favorite of Napoleon and many other military leaders.*

*A much disliked chore even in fair weather — a lone Union soldier walks his post in the bitter cold at Nashville.*

A forerunner of Father Francis Patrick Duffy, heroic Chaplain of the famous 69th New York Regiment in World War I, says Mass for the Shamrock Regiment of the 1860's. Most Civil War regiments had a chaplain.

A contribution to camp religious life, the 50th New York Engineers constructed this church for their comrades at Petersburg.

Newspaper correspondents like these from the New York Herald kept the public well informed, though they often revealed valuable military information to the Confederacy. The New York paper usually reached the Confederate War Department on the day following publication.

With the technique of photo-engraving yet to be developed, war scenes for newspapers and magazines had to be drawn and reproduced from woodcuts. Artists such as A. R. Waud, shown here at Gettysburg, vividly depicted the events for Harper's Weekly.

The Civil War as it appeared back home. It was almost 40 years before the public saw the thousands of photographs taken by Mathew Brady and his contemporaries.

In a desperate attempt to raise the Federal blockade of Southern ports, the Confederate Navy built the first ironclad. More than a dozen of these rams, all similar to the Albemarle (pictured above), were constructed.

At first, ironclads were scoffed at by Federal naval authorities, but the monitors, styled "iron coffins", proved their worth in battle with the river navies. By 1865 fifty-eight of the turreted vessels had been built, some of which became seagoing.

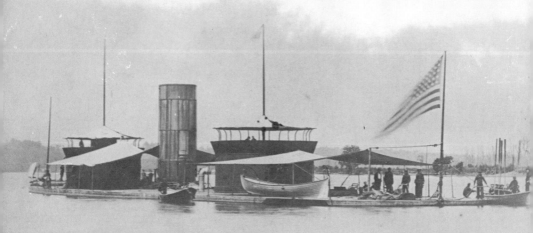

With untiring vigilance, steam-powered gunboats like the Mendota plied the Southern coastline to enforce the blockade against Confederate trade with England and France.

The C.S.S. Hunley, a completely submersible craft, was hand-propelled by a crew of eight. The 25-foot submarine sank off Charleston along with her first and only victim, the U.S.S. Housatonic.

Steam-powered torpedo boats of the Confederate Navy were capable of partially submerging with only their stacks showing. These tiny "Davids", named after the Biblical warior, could be either manned or remotely controlled from shore.

CAPTAIN OF ARTILLERY. U.S.ARMY.
FULL DRESS.

COLONEL OF INFANTRY. U.S.ARMY.
FULL DRESS.

BRIG. GENERAL. U.S.ARMY.
FULL DRESS.

LIEUT. GENERAL. U.S.ARMY.
UNDRESS.

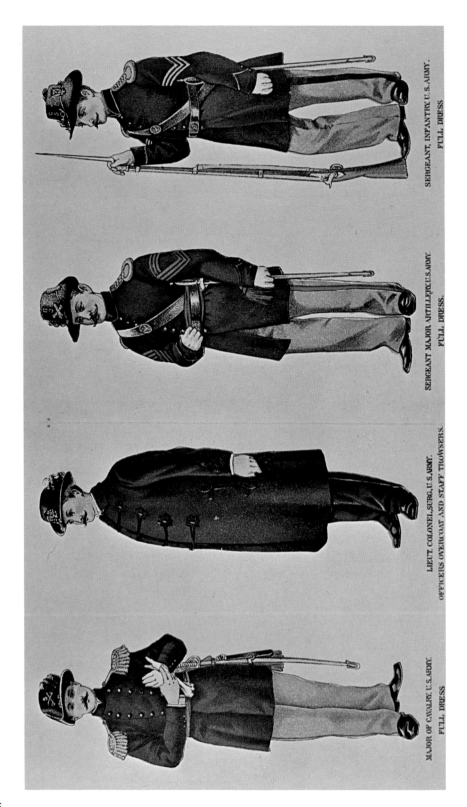

MAJOR OF CAVALRY, U.S. ARMY.
FULL DRESS.

LIEUT. COLONEL, SURG, U.S. ARMY.
OFFICERS OVERCOAT AND STAFF TROWSERS.

SERGEANT MAJOR ARTILLERY, U.S. ARMY.
FULL DRESS.

SERGEANT, INFANTRY, U.S. ARMY.
FULL DRESS.

GREAT COAT
FOR ALL MOUNTED MEN.

PRIVATE, LIGHT ARTILLERY, U.S.ARMY.
FULL DRESS.

CORPORAL, CAVALRY, U.S.ARMY.
FULL DRESS.

PRIVATE, U.S. INFANTRY.
FATIGUE MARCHING ORDER.

UNITED STATES UNIFORMS IN THE CIVIL WAR

REG. CAVALRY PRIVATE. GEN. GRANT'S UNIFORM. ARTILLERY LINE OFFICER. DURYEAS ZOUAVE. HAWKIN'S ZOUAVE. REG. INFANTRY PRIVATE. DURYEAS ZOUAVE LINE OFFICER. CAMPAIGN UNIFORM INFANTRY. REG. ARTILLERY PRIVATE. INFANTRY OVER COAT.

· CONFEDERATE UNIFORMS ·

NORTH CAROLINA REG. INFANTRY WASHINGTON MONTGOMERY FIELD OFFICER GEN. LEE'S UNIFORM. REG. CAVALRY LOUISIANA LOUISIANA REG. ARTILLERY
MILITIA. PRIVATE. ARTILLERY. TRUE BLUE. OF INFANTRY. PRIVATE. TIGER. ZOUAVE. PRIVATE.

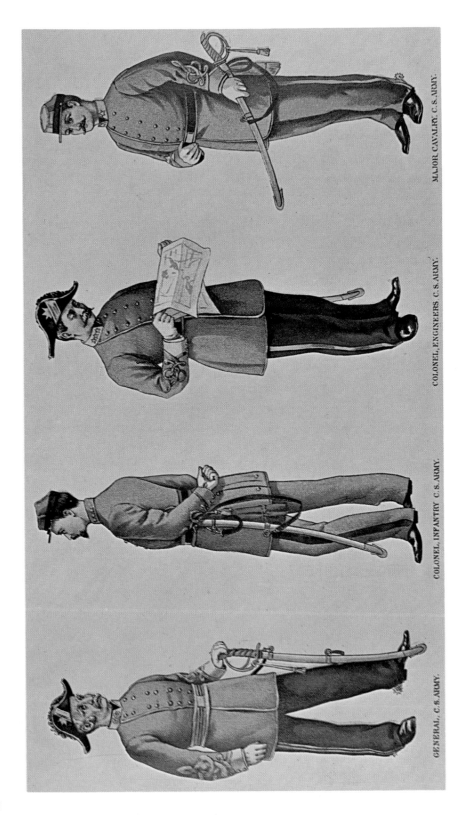

GENERAL, C. S. ARMY.

COLONEL, INFANTRY C. S. ARMY.

COLONEL, ENGINEERS C. S. ARMY.

MAJOR, CAVALRY, C. S. ARMY.

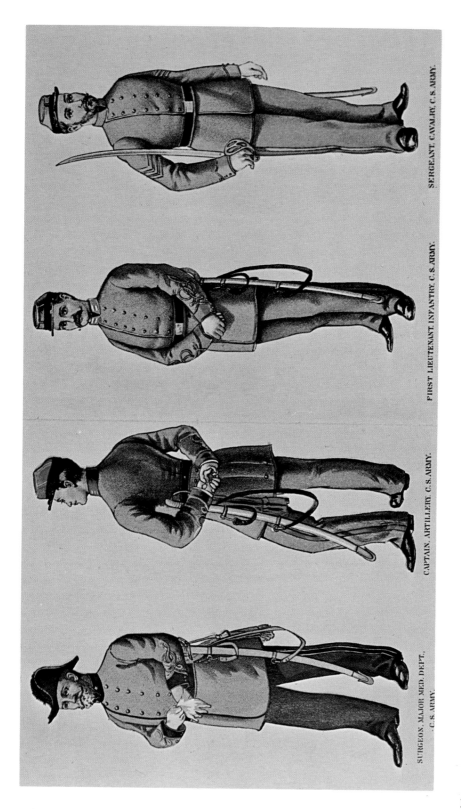

SURGEON, MAJOR MED. DEPT.,
C. S. ARMY.

CAPTAIN, ARTILLERY, C. S. ARMY.

FIRST LIEUTENANT, INFANTRY, C. S. ARMY.

SERGEANT, CAVALRY, C. S. ARMY.

39

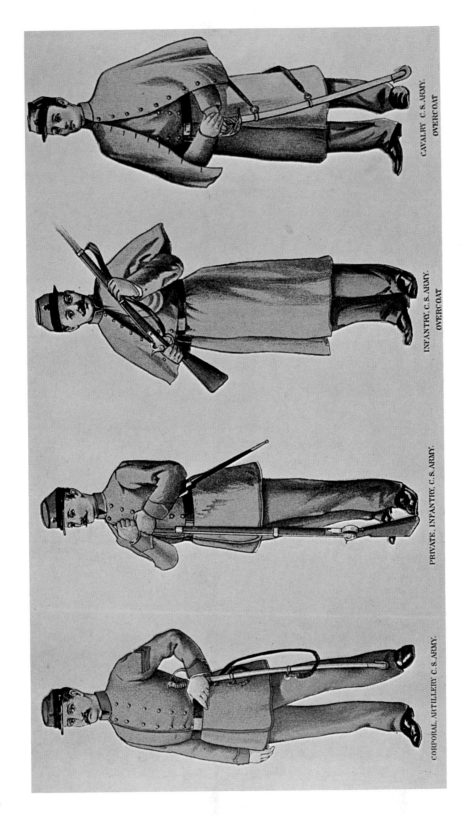

CAVALRY C. S. ARMY.
OVERCOAT

INFANTRY. C. S. ARMY.
OVERCOAT

PRIVATE, INFANTRY. C. S. ARMY.

CORPORAL. ARTILLERY C.S. ARMY.

In 1864 nearly 4,000 wagons traveled with Meade's Army of the Potomac, each capable of carrying 2,500 pounds of supplies. During one year the Federal Army purchased 14,500 wagons and captured an additional 2,000.

41

"The muscles of his brawny arms are strong as iron bands. . ." Union Army black-smiths had to shoe nearly 500 new horses and mules daily.

*An old timer that traveled many miles of Virginia road with a busy and tireless man — General U. S. Grant.*

42

*General Lee had hoped that Virginia's numerous streams and rivers would delay Grant's advance, but Federal engineers with portable pontoon bridges kept the army at Lee's heels.*

This "cornstalk" bridge over Potomac Creek near Fredericksburg was built by the Military Railroad construction corps from 204,000 feet of standing timber in nine days.

In one year (1864-1865) the Federal Military Railroad, with 365 engines and 4,203 cars, delivered over 5 million tons of supplies to the armies in the field.

*Schooners piled high with cartridge boxes lie in the placid waters off Hampton Roads. In 1865 hundreds of Union troops and supplies were moved by ocean transports, chartered at a daily cost of $92,000.*

*Federal ships crowd the magazine wharf at City Point with equipment and supplies for army wagons from Petersburg. Twenty per cent of the total supply tonnage was transported by water.*

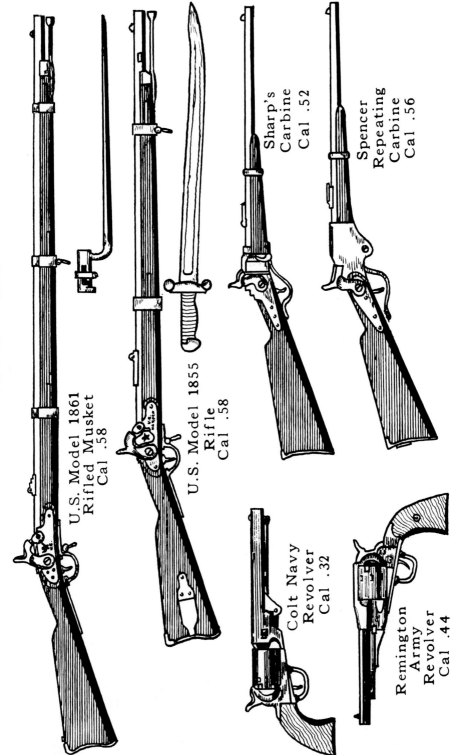

CIVIL WAR SMALL ARMS

by William H. Price

U.S. Model 1861 Rifled Musket Cal .58

U.S. Model 1855 Rifle Cal .58

Sharp's Carbine Cal .52

Spencer Repeating Carbine Cal .56

Colt Navy Revolver Cal .32

Remington Army Revolver Cal .44

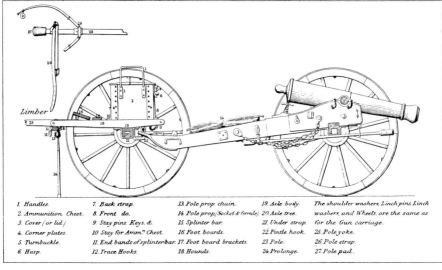

| | | | | |
|---|---|---|---|---|
| 1. Handles. | 7. Back strap. | 13. Pole prop chain. | 19. Axle body. | The shoulder washers, Linch pins, Linch |
| 2. Ammunition Chest. | 8. Front do. | 14. Pole prop (Socket & ferrule). | 20. Axle tree. | washers, and Wheels, are the same as |
| 3. Cover (or lid.) | 9. Stay pins, Keys, &. | 15. Splinter bar. | 21. Under strap. | for the Gun carriage. |
| 4. Corner plates. | 10. Stay for Amm.ⁿ Chest. | 16. Foot boards. | 22. Pintle hook. | 25. Pole yoke. |
| 5. Turnbuckle. | 11. End bands of splinterbar. | 17. Foot board brackets. | 23. Pole. | 26. Pole strap. |
| 6. Hasp. | 12. Trace Hooks. | 18. Hounds. | 24. Prolonge. | 27. Pole pad. |

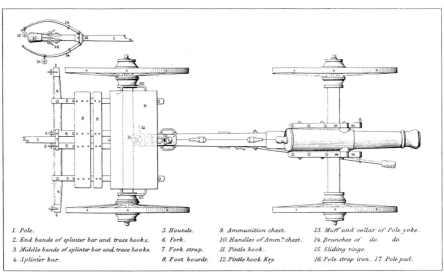

| | | | |
|---|---|---|---|
| 1. Pole. | 5. Hounds. | 9. Ammunition chest. | 13. Muff and collar of Pole yoke. |
| 2. End bands of splinter bar and trace hooks. | 6. Fork. | 10. Handles of Amm.ⁿ chest. | 14. Branches of do. do. |
| 3. Middle bands of splinter bar and trace hooks. | 7. Fork strap. | 11. Pintle hook. | 15. Sliding rings. |
| 4. Splinter bar. | 8. Foot boards. | 12. Pintle hook Key. | 16. Pole strap iron. 17. Pole pad. |

## MAXIMUM EFFECTIVE RANGE IN YARDS

| | |
|---|---:|
| 12-Pounder Howitzer | 1,070 |
| 6 & 12-Pounder Field Guns | 1,200 |
| 13-Inch Siege Mortar | 3,520 |
| 10-Pounder Parrott Rifle | 5,000 |
| 10-Inch Columbiad Siege Gun | 5,650 |
| 30-Pounder Parrott Rifle | 8,450 |
| 12-Pounder Whitworth Rifle | 8,800 |

### TYPICAL GUNNER'S TABLE

12-Pounder Field Gun                    Powder Charge 2.5 lbs.

| Range (yards) | 600 | 700 | 800 | 900 | 1,000 | 1,100 | 1,200 |
|---|---|---|---|---|---|---|---|
| Muzzle Elevation | 1° | 1°45' | 2° | 2°15' | 2°30' | 3° | 3°30' |
| Fuse Setting (sec.) | 1.75 | 2.50 | 2.75 | 3.00 | 3.25 | 4.00 | 4.50 |

A 15-inch Rodman smoothbore, one of the largest guns mounted during the war, stands as a silent sentry guarding the Potomac at Alexandria, Virginia.

The Parrott Rifle, recognizable by the wrought iron jacket reinforcing its breech, was one of the first rifled field guns used by the U.S. Army.

Chevaux-de-frise, made of logs pierced by sharp stakes, line the Georgia countryside. Confederate defensive measures such as this were effective in stopping cavalry and preventing surprise frontal attacks by infantry.

The Union military telegraph corps strung more than 15,000 miles of wire during the war. In one year, the Northern armies kept the wires alive with nearly 1.8 million messages. Galvanic batteries transported by wagon furnished the electricity.

Flag signals from natural elevations and signal towers could be seen as far as 20 miles on a clear day. Military information was often abtained by signalmen on both sides who copied each others flag messages and tapped telegraph lines.

*Balloon observation on the battlefield was made possible by the portable gas generator. Here Professor T.S.C. Lowe's balloon is inflated by mobile generators in front of Richmond in 1862.*

52

*Dodging Confederate shells which whizzed dangerously close to the Intrepid, Professor Lowe telegraphed information on emplacements directly from his balloon and made sketches of the approach routes to Richmond.*

Faulty intelligence furnished by detective Allan Pinkerton (seated in rear) and his agents misled General George McClellan during the Peninsula Campaign. The Pinkerton organization was later replaced by a more efficient military intelligence bureau.

A. D. Lytle, a Baton Rouge photographer, provided valuable intelligence to Confederate commanders. His photographs, like this one posed by the 1st Indiana Heavy Artillery, revealed the strength and condition of Union organizations.

Artillerymen soften an objective for the infantry. Although field artillery was used extensively, it frightened and demoralized more men than it wounded. Only 20 per cent of the battle casualties can be attributed to the artillery.

Assaults on fortified positions were costly, but here at Petersburg war-weary infantrymen await their turn for another charge against the Confederate works. Fourteen out of every hundred would fall.

55

One of an estimated 584,000 Union and Confederate soldiers wounded during the war. Of this number, over 80,000 died.

The Union ambulance corps provided one ambulance for every 150 men during the Wilderness Campaign. In one convoy of 813 ambulances, over 7,000 sick and wounded were transported to the hospital in Fredericksburg.

Amputees, like these Union soldiers who survived the surgeon's scalpel, would never forget the traumatic ordeal. Most wounded went through surgery while fully conscious with but a little morphine, when available, to deaden the pain.

A floating palace with bathrooms and laundry, the hospital ship Red Rover gave many sick and wounded a better chance for life than they would have had in the crowded field hospitals.

Carver Hospital, where thousands of stricken soldiers recovered. Walt Whitman and Louisa May Alcott nursed many sick and wounded in similar Washington hospitals.

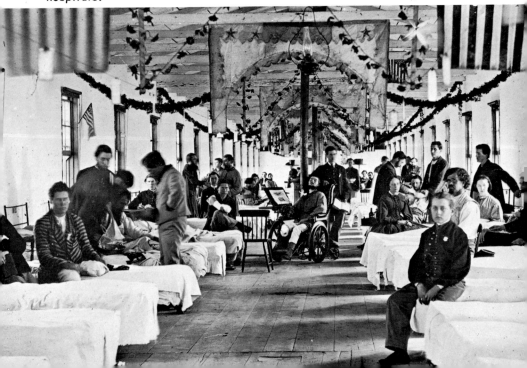

The much-publicized Andersonville prison. The declaration by Union authorities that medicine was a contraband of war and their unwillingness to exchange prisoners contributed to the deplorable prison deaths. Prisoners didn't fare better in the North. Camp Douglas, Illinois, had the highest death rate of all Civil war prisons — 10 per cent of its prisoners died in one month.

Unknown warriors at Cold Harbor awaited a soldier's burial that never came. Two years later the armies returned to the same field of battle to find those who were forgotten — still waiting.

60

Boys volunteered for a man's job. This Confederate lad gave his last full measure.

"The muffled drum's sad roll has beat
   The soldier's last tattoo;
No more on Life's parade shall meet
   The brave and fallen few.

On Fame's eternal camping-ground
   Their silent tents are spread
And Glory guards, with solemn round,
   The bivouac of the dead."
      —THEODORE O'HARA

61

62 *Richmond 1865 — Gaunt remains cast their shadow over the former Confederate capital. The rampaging fire, started during the evacuation, leveled the waterfront and the business district.*

Charleston, South Carolina, shows the scars of modern warfare. The concept of tatal war introduced during the 1860's carried destruction beyond the battle- 63 field.

*The home of Wilmer McLean at Appomattox.  Here the tragic drama closed at 3:45 on Palm Sunday afternoon, April 9, 1865.*

64

THE SURRENDER AT APPOMATTOX; BASED UPON THE LITHOGRAPH CALLED "THE DAWN OF PEACE." BY PERMISSION OF W. H. STELLE.

2. General Robert E. Lee.  1. Colonel Charles Marshall, of General Lee's Staff.  8. Lieutenant-General Ulysses S. Grant.  15. Major-General Philip H. Sheridan.  7. Major-General Edward O. C. Ord.  14. Brevet Major-General Rufus Ingalls.  10. Brigadier-General John A. Rawlins, Chief-of-Staff; other members of General Grant's Staff: 4. Major-General Seth Williams.  12. Brevet Major-General John G. Barnard.  9. Colonel Horace Porter.  3. Colonel Orville E. Babcock.  5. Colonel Ely S. Parker.  6. Colonel Theodore S. Bowers.  11. Colonel Frederick T. Dent.  13. Colonel Adam Badeau.

*Pennsylvania Avenue — host to the Armies of Grant and Sherman during the Grand Review.*

The last reunion of Blue and Gray at Gettysburg. The victories and the defeats . . . they have become a common property and a common responsibility of the American people.

# Losses in Killed, Wounded, and Missing in Engagements, Etc.,

## Where the Total was Five Hundred or more on the side of the Union Troops. Confederate Losses given are generally based on Estimates.

| No. | Date. | Name. | Union Loss. Killed. | Wounded. | Missing. | Total. | Confederate Loss—Total. |
|---|---|---|---|---|---|---|---|
| | **1861.** | | | | | | |
| 1 | July 21................... | Bull Run, Va........................... | 481 | 1,011 | 1,460 | 2,952 | 1,752 |
| 2 | August 10 ............. | Wilson's Creek, Mo..................... | 223 | 721 | 291 | 1,235 | 1,095 |
| 3 | September 12 to 20........ | Lexington, Mo.......................... | 42 | 108 | 1,624 | 1,774 | 100 |
| 4 | October 21................ | Ball's Bluff, Va....................... | 223 | 226 | 445 | 894 | 302 |
| 5 | November 7............... | Belmont, Mo............................ | 90 | 173 | 235 | 498 | 966 |
| | **1862.** | | | | | | |
| 6 | February 14 to 16.......... | Fort Donelson, Tenn.................... | 446 | 1,735 | 150 | 2,331 | 15,067 |
| 7 | March 6 to 8.............. | Pea Ridge, Ark........................ | 203 | 972 | 174 | 1,349 | 5,200 |
| 8 | March 14................. | New-Berne, N. C....................... | 91 | 466 | ....... | 557 | 583 |
| 9 | March 23................. | Winchester, Va........................ | 103 | 440 | 24 | 567 | 691 |
| 10 | April 6 and 7............. | Shiloh, Tenn.......................... | 1,735 | 7,882 | 3,956 | 13,573 | 10,699 |
| 11 | May 5.................... | Williamsburg, Va...................... | 456 | 1,400 | 372 | 2,228 | 1,000 |
| 12 | May 23................... | Front Royal, Va....................... | 32 | 122 | 750 | 904 | ....... |
| 13 | May 25................... | Winchester, Va........................ | 38 | 155 | 711 | 904 | |
| 14 | May 31 to June 1.......... | Seven Pines and Fair Oaks, Va........ | 890 | 3,627 | 1,222 | 5,739 | 7,997 |
| 15 | June 8................... | Cross Keys, Va........................ | 125 | 500 | ....... | 625 | 287 |
| 16 | June 9................... | Fort Republic, Va..................... | 67 | 361 | 574 | 1,002 | 657 |
| 17 | June 16.................. | Secessionville, James Island, S. C.... | 85 | 472 | 128 | 685 | 204 |
| 18 | June 25.................. | Oak Grove, Va......................... | 51 | 401 | 64 | 516 | 541 |
| 19 | June 26 to July 1.......... | Seven days' retreat; includes Mechanicsville, Gaines' Mills, Chickahominy, Peach Orchard, Savage Station, Charles City Cross Roads, and Malvern Hill ....................... | 1,582 | 7,709 | 5,958 | 15,249 | 17,583 |
| 20 | July 13.................. | Murfreesboro', Tenn................... | 33 | 62 | 800 | 895 | 150 |
| 21 | August 8................. | Cedar Mountain, Va.................... | 450 | 660 | 290 | 1,400 | 1,307 |
| 22 | July 20 to September 20.... | Guerrilla campaign in Missouri; includes Porter's and Poindexter's Guerrillas............ | 77 | 156 | 347 | 580 | 2,866 |
| 23 | August 28 and 29.......... | Groveton and Gainesville, Va.......... | ........ | ....... | ....... | 7,000 | 7,000 |
| 24 | August 30................ | Bull Run, Va. (2d)................... | 800. | 4,000 | 3,000 | 7,800 | 3,700 |
| 25 | August 30................ | Richmond, Ky.......................... | 200 | 700 | 4,000 | 4,900 | 750 |
| 26 | September 1.............. | Chantilly, Va......................... | ........ | ....... | ....... | 1,300 | 800 |
| 27 | September 12 to 15........ | Harper's Ferry, Va.................... | 80 | 120 | 11,583 | 11,783 | 500 |
| 28 | September 14.. .......... | Turner's and Crampton's Gaps, South Mountain, Md ........................... | 443 | 1,806 | 76 | 2,325 | 4,343 |
| 29 | September 14 to 16........ | Munfordsville, Ky..................... | 50 | ....... | 3,566 | 3,616 | 714 |
| 30 | September 17............. | Antietam, Md.......................... | 2,010 | 9,416 | 1,043 | 12,469 | 25,899 |
| 31 | September 19 to 20........ | Iuka, Miss............................ | 144 | 598 | 40 | 782 | 1,516 |
| 32 | October 3 and 4........... | Corinth, Miss......................... | 315 | 1,812 | 232 | 2,359 | 14,221 |
| **33** | October 5................ | **Big Hatchie River, Miss.**........... | ........ | ....... | ....... | 500 | 400 |
| 34 | October 8................ | Perryville, Ky........................ | 916 | 2,943 | 489 | 4,348 | 7,000 |
| 35 | December 7.............. | Prairie Grove, Ark.................... | 167 | 798 | 183 | 1,148 | 1,500 |
| 36 | December 7.............. | Hartsville, Tenn...................... | 55 | ....... | 1,800 | 1,855 | 149 |
| 37 | December 12 to 18.......... | Foster's expedition to Goldsboro', N. C ...... | 90 | 478 | 9 | 577 | 739 |
| 38 | December 13.. .......... | Fredericksburg, Va.................... | 1,180 | 9,028 | 2,145 | 12,353 | 4,576 |
| 39 | December 20............. | Holly Springs, Miss................... | ........ | ....... | 1,000 | 1,000 | ....... |
| 40 | December 27............. | Elizabethtown, Ky..................... | ........ | ....... | 500 | 500 | |
| 41 | December 28 and 29........ | Chickasaw Bayou, Vicksburg, Miss...... | 191 | 982 | 756 | 1,929 | 207 |
| 42 | Dec. 31, 1862, to Jan. 2, 1863. | Stone's River, Tenn................... | 1,533 | 7,245 | 2,800 | 11,578 | 25,560 |
| | **1863.** | | | | | | |
| 43 | January 1................ | Galveston, Texas...................... | ........ | ....... | 600 | 600 | 50 |
| 44 | January 11............... | Fort Hindman, Arkansas Post, Ark..... | 129 | 831 | 17 | 977 | 5,500 |
| 45 | March 4 and 5............ | Thompson's Station, Tenn.............. | 100 | 300 | 1,306 | 1,706 | 600 |
| 46 | April 27 to May 3.......... | Streight's raid from Tuscumbia, Ala., to Rome, Ga................................ | 12 | 69 | 1,466 | 1,547 | ....... |
| 47 | May 1.................... | Port Gibson, Miss..................... | 130 | 718 | 5 | 853 | 1,650 |
| 48 | May 1 to 4............... | Chancellorsville, Va.................. | 1,512 | 9,518 | 5,000 | 16,030 | 12,281 |
| 49 | May 16................... | Champion Mills, Miss................. | 426 | 1,842 | 189 | 2,457 | 4,300 |
| 50 | May 18 to July 4.......... | Siege of Vicksburg, Miss.............. | 545 | 3,688 | 303 | 4,536 | 31,277 |
| 51 | May 27 to July 9.......... | Siege of Port Hudson, La.............. | 500 | 2,500 | ....... | 3,000 | 7,208 |
| 52 | June 6 to 8.............. | Milliken's Bend, La. . ........... . | 154 | 223 | 115 | 492 | 725 |
| 53 | June 9................... | Beverly Ford and Brandy Station, Va......... | ........ | ....... | ....... | 500 | 700 |
| 54 | June 13 to 15............. | Winchester, Va........................ | ........ | ....... | 3,000 | 3,000 | 850 |
| 55 | June 23 to 30............. | Rosecrans' campaign from Murfreesboro' to Tullahoma, Tenn..... ............. | 85 | 462 | 13 | 560 | 1,634 |
| 56 | July 1 to 3.............. | Gettysburg, Pa........................ | 2,834 | 13,709 | 6,643 | 23,186 | 31,621 |
| 57 | July 9 to 16............. | Jackson, Miss......................... | 100 | 800 | 100 | 1,000 | 1,339 |

| No. | Date | Name | Union Loss. | | | | Confederate Loss—Total. |
|---|---|---|---|---|---|---|---|
| | | | Killed. | Wounded. | Missing. | Total. | |
| 58 | July 18 | Second assault on Fort Wagner, S. C. | | | | 1,500 | 174 |
| 59 | September 19 to 20 | Chickamauga, Ga. | 1,644 | 9,262 | 4,945 | 15,851 | 17,804 |
| 60 | November 3 | Grand Coteau, La. | 26 | 124 | 576 | 726 | 445 |
| 61 | November 6 | Rogersville, Tenn. | 5 | 12 | 650 | 667 | 30 |
| 62 | November 23 to 25 | Chattanooga, Tenn.; includes Orchard Knob, Lookout Mountain, and Missionary Ridge | 757 | 4,529 | 330 | 5,616 | 8,684 |
| 63 | November 26 to 28 | Operations at Mine Run, Va. | 100 | 400 | | 500 | 500 |
| 64 | December 14 | Bean's Station, Tenn. | | | | 700 | 900 |
| | **1864.** | | | | | | |
| 65 | February 20 | Olustee, Fla. | 193 | 1,175 | 460 | 1,828 | 500 |
| 66 | April 8 | Sabine Cross Roads, La. | 200 | 900 | 1,800 | 2,900 | 1,500 |
| 67 | April 9 | Pleasant Hills, La. | 100 | 700 | 300 | 1,100 | 2,000 |
| 68 | April 12 | Fort Pillow, Tenn. | 350 | 60 | 164 | 574 | 80 |
| 69 | April 17 to 20 | Plymouth, N. C. | 20 | 80 | 1,500 | 1,600 | 500 |
| 70 | April 30 | Jenkins' Ferry, Saline River, Ark. | 200 | 955 | | 1,155 | 1,100 |
| 71 | May 5 to 7 | Wilderness, Va. | 5,597 | 21,463 | 10,677 | 37,737 | 11,400 |
| 72 | May 5 to 9 | Rocky Face Ridge, Ga.; includes Tunnel Hill, Mill Creek Gap, Buzzard Roost, Snake Creek Gap, and near Dalton | 200 | 637 | | 837 | 600 |
| 73 | May 8 to 18 | Spottsylvania Court House, Va.; includes engagements on the Fredericksburg Road, Laurel Hill, and Nye River | 4,177 | 19,687 | 2,577 | 26,461 | **9,000** |
| 74 | May 9 to 10 | Swift Creek, Va. | 90 | 400 | | 490 | 500 |
| 75 | May 9 to 10 | Cloyd's Mountain and New River Bridge, Va. | 126 | 585 | 34 | 745 | 900 |
| 76 | May 12 to 16 | Fort Darling, Drewry's Bluff, Va. | 422 | 2,380 | 210 | 3,012 | 2,500 |
| 77 | May 13 to 16 | Resaca, Ga. | 600 | 2,147 | | 2,747 | 2,800 |
| 78 | May 15 | New Market, Va. | 120 | 560 | 240 | 920 | 405 |
| 79 | May 16 to 30 | Bermuda Hundred, Va. | 200 | 1,000 | | 1,200 | 3,000 |
| 80 | May 23 to 27 | North Anna River, Va. | 223 | 1,460 | 290 | 1,973 | 2,000 |
| 81 | May 25 to June 4 | Dallas, Ga. | | | | 2,400 | 3,000 |
| 82 | June 1 to 12 | Cold Harbor, Va. | 1,905 | 10,570 | 2,456 | 14,931 | 1,700 |
| 83 | June 5 | Piedmont, Va. | 130 | 650 | | 780 | 2,970 |
| 84 | June 9 to 30 | Kenesaw Mountain, Ga.; includes Pine Mountain, Pine Knob, Golgotha, Culp's House, general assault, June 27th : McAfee's Cross Roads, Lattemore's Mills and Powder Springs | 1,370 | 6,500 | 800 | 8,670 | 4,600 |
| 85 | June 10 | Brice's Cross Roads, near Guntown, Miss. | 223 | 394 | 1,623 | 2,240 | 606 |
| 86 | June 10 | Kellar's Bridge, Licking River, Ky. | 13 | 54 | 700 | 767 | |
| 87 | June 11 and 12 | Trevellian Station, Central Railroad, Va. | 85 | 490 | 160 | 735 | 370 |
| 88 | June 15 to 19 | Petersburg, Va.; includes Baylor's Farm, Walthal, and Weir Bottom Church | 1,298 | 7,474 | 1,814 | 10,586 | |
| 89 | June 17 and 18 | Lynchburg, Va. | 100 | 500 | 400 | 700 | 200 |
| 90 | June 20 to 30 | Trenches in front of Petersburg, Va. | 112 | 506 | 800 | 1,418 | |
| 91 | June 22 to 30 | Wilson's raid on the Weldon Railroad, Va. | 76 | 265 | 700 | 1,041 | 300 |
| 92 | June 22 and 23 | Weldon Railroad, Va. | 604 | 2,494 | 2,217 | 5,315 | 500 |
| 93 | June 27 | Kenesaw Mountain, general assault. See No. 2,345 | | | | 3,000 | 608 |
| 94 | July 1 to 31 | Front of Petersburg, Va.; losses at the Crater and Deep Bottom not included | 419 | 2,076 | 1,200 | 3,695 | |
| 95 | July 6 to 10 | Chattahoochee River, Ga. | 80 | 450 | 200 | 730 | 600 |
| 96 | July 9 | Monocacy, Md. | 90 | 579 | 1,290 | 1,959 | 400 |
| 97 | July 13 to 15 | Tupelo, Miss.; includes Harrisburg and Old Town Creek | 85 | 563 | | 648 | 700 |
| 98 | July 20 | Peach Tree Creek, Ga. | 300 | 1,410 | | 1,710 | 4,796 |
| 99 | July 22 | Atlanta, Ga.; Hood's first sortie | 500 | 2,141 | 1,000 | 3,641 | 8,499 |
| 100 | July 24 | Winchester, Va. | | | | 1,200 | 600 |
| 101 | July 26 to 31 | Stoneman's raid to Macon, Ga. | | 100 | 900 | 1,000 | |
| 102 | July 26 to 31 | McCook's raid to Lovejoy Station, Ga. | | 100 | 500 | 600 | |
| 103 | July 28 | Ezra Chapel, Atlanta, Ga.; second sortie | 100 | 600 | | 700 | 4,642 |
| 104 | July 30 | Mine explosion at Petersburg, Va. | 419 | 1,679 | 1,910 | 4,008 | 1,200 |
| 105 | August 1 to 31 | Trenches before Petersburg, Va. | 87 | 484 | | 571 | |
| 106 | August 14 to 18 | Strawberry Plains, Deep Bottom Run, Va. | 400 | 1,755 | 1,400 | 3,555 | 1,100 |
| 107 | August 18, 19 and 21 | Six Mile House, Weldon Railroad, Va. | 212 | 1,155 | 3,176 | 4,543 | 4,000 |
| 108 | August 21 | Summit Point, Va. | | | | 600 | 400 |
| 109 | August 25 | Ream's Station, Va. | 127 | 546 | 1,769 | 2,442 | 1,500 |
| 110 | August 31 to September 1 | Jonesboro', Ga. | | | 1,149 | 1,149 | 2,000 |
| 111 | May 5 to September 8 | Campaign in Northern Georgia, from Chattanooga, Tenn., to Atlanta, Ga. | 5,284 | 26,129 | 5,786 | 37,199 | |
| 112 | September 1 to October 30 | Trenches before Petersburg, Va. | 170 | 822 | 812 | 1,804 | 1,000 |
| 113 | September 19 | Opequan, Winchester, Va. | 653 | 3,719 | 618 | 4,990 | 5,500 |
| 114 | September 23 | Athens, Ala. | | | | 950 | 30 |
| 115 | September 24 to October 28 | Price's invasion of Missouri; includes a number of engagements | 170 | 336 | | 506 | |
| 116 | September 28 to 30 | New Market Heights, Va. | 400 | 2,029 | | 2,429 | 2,000 |
| 117 | September 30 to October 1 | Preble's Farm, Poplar Springs Church, Va. | 141 | 788 | 1,756 | 2,685 | 900 |

| No. | DATE. | NAME. | UNION LOSS. Killed. | UNION LOSS. Wounded. | UNION LOSS. Missing. | UNION LOSS. Total. | CONFEDERATE Loss—Total. |
|---|---|---|---|---|---|---|---|
| 118 | October 5 | Allatoona, Ga. | 142 | 352 | 212 | 706 | 1,142 |
| 119 | October 19 | Cedar Creek, Va. | 588 | 3,516 | 1,891 | 5,995 | 4,200 |
| 120 | October 27 | Hatcher's Run, South Side Railroad, Va. | 156 | 1,047 | 699 | 1,902 | 1,000 |
| 121 | October 27 and 28 | Fair Oaks, near Richmond, Va. | 120 | 783 | 400 | 1,303 | 451 |
| 122 | November 28 | Fort Kelly, New Creek, West Va. | ...... | ...... | 700 | 700 | 5 |
| 123 | November 30 | Franklin, Tenn. | 189 | 1,033 | 1,104 | 2,326 | 6.252 |
| 124 | November 30 | Honey Hill, Broad River, S. C. | 66 | 645 | ...... | 711 | ...... |
| 125 | December 6 to 9 | Deveaux's Neck, S. C. | 39 | 390 | 200 | 629 | 400 |
| 126 | December 15 and 16 | Nashville, Tenn. | 400 | 1,740 | ...... | 2,140 | 15,000 |
| | **1865.** | | | | | | |
| 127 | January 11 | Beverly, West Va. | 5 | 20 | 583 | 608 | ...... |
| 128 | January 13 to 15 | Fort Fisher, N. C. | 184 | 749 | 22 | 955 | 2,483 |
| 129 | February 5 to 7 | Dabney's Mills, Hatcher's Run, Va. | 232 | 1,062 | 186 | 1,480 | 1,200 |
| 130 | March 8 to 10 | Wilcox's Bridge, Wise's Fork, N. C. | 80 | 421 | 600 | 1,101 | 1,500 |
| 131 | March 16 | Averysboro', N. C. | 77 | 477 | ...... | 554 | 865 |
| 132 | March 19 to 21 | Bentonville, N. C. | 191 | 1,168 | 287 | 1,646 | 2,825 |
| 133 | March 25 | Fort Steedman, in front of Petersburg, Va. | 68 | 337 | 506 | 911 | 2,681 |
| 134 | March 25 | Petersburg, Va. | 103 | 864 | 209 | 1,176 | 834 |
| 135 | March 26 to April 8 | Spanish Fort, Ala. | 100 | 695 | ...... | 795 | 552 |
| 136 | March 22 to April 24 | Wilson's raid from Chickasaw, Ala., to Macon, Ga.; includes a number of engagements. | 99 | 598 | 28 | 725 | 8,020 |
| 137 | March 31 | Boydton and White Oak Roads, Va. | 177 | 1,134 | 556 | 1,867 | 1,235 |
| 138 | April 1 | Five Forks, Va. | 124 | 706 | 54 | 884 | 8,500 |
| 139 | April 2 | Fall of Petersburg, Va. | 296 | 2,565 | 500 | 3,361 | 3,000 |
| 140 | April 6 | Sailor's Creek, Va. | 166 | 1,014 | ...... | 1,180 | 7,000 |
| 141 | April 6 | High Bridge, Appomattox River, Va. | 10 | 31 | 1,000 | 1,041 | ...... |
| 142 | April 7 | Farmville, Va. | ...... | ...... | ...... | 655 | ...... |
| 143 | April 9 | Fort Blakely, Ala. | 113 | 516 | ...... | 629 | 2,900 |
| 144 | April 9 | Surrender of Lee. | ...... | ...... | ...... | ...... | 26,000 |
| 145 | April 26 | Johnston surrendered. | ...... | ...... | ...... | ...... | 29,924 |
| 146 | May 4 | Taylor surrendered. | ...... | ...... | ...... | ...... | 10,000 |
| 147 | May 10 | Sam Jones surrendered. | ...... | ...... | ...... | ...... | 8,000 |
| 148 | May 11 | Jeff Thompson surrendered. | ...... | ...... | ...... | ...... | 7,454 |
| 149 | May 26 | Kirby Smith surrendered. | ...... | ...... | ...... | ...... | 20,000 |

# Statement of the Number of Engagements

## IN THE SEVERAL STATES AND TERRITORIES DURING EACH YEAR OF THE WAR.

| STATES AND TERRITORIES. | 1861 | 1862 | 1863 | 1864 | 1865 | Total. | STATES AND TERRITORIES. | 1861 | 1862 | 1863 | 1864 | 1865 | Total. |
|---|---|---|---|---|---|---|---|---|---|---|---|---|---|
| New York, | .. | .. | 1 | .. | .. | 1 | Illinois | .. | .. | .. | 1 | .. | 1 |
| Pennsylvania, | .. | .. | 8 | 1 | .. | 9 | Missouri, | 65 | 95 | 43 | 41 | .. | 244 |
| Maryland, | 3 | 9 | 10 | 8 | .. | 30 | Minnesota, | .. | 5 | 1 | .. | .. | 6 |
| Dist. of Columbia, | .. | .. | .. | 1 | .. | 1 | California, | .. | 1 | 4 | 1 | .. | 6 |
| West Virginia, | 29 | 114 | 17 | 19 | 1 | 80 | Kansas, | .. | .. | 2 | 5 | .. | 7 |
| Virginia, | 30 | 40 | 116 | 205 | 28 | 519 | Oregon, | .. | .. | .. | 3 | 1 | 4 |
| North Carolina, | 2 | 27 | 18 | 10 | 28 | 85 | Nevada, | .. | .. | .. | 2 | .. | 2 |
| South Carolina, | 2 | 10 | 17 | 9 | 22 | 60 | Washington Ter. | .. | .. | 1 | .. | .. | 1 |
| Georgia, | .. | 2 | 8 | 92 | 6 | 108 | Utah, | .. | .. | .. | 1 | .. | 1 |
| Florida, | 3 | 3 | 4 | 17 | 5 | 32 | New Mexico, | 3 | 5 | 7 | 4 | .. | 19 |
| Alabama, | .. | 10 | 12 | 32 | 24 | 78 | Nebraska, | .. | .. | 2 | .. | .. | 2 |
| Mississippi, | .. | 42 | 76 | 67 | 1 | 186 | Colorado, | .. | .. | .. | 4 | .. | 4 |
| Louisiana, | 1 | 11 | 54 | 50 | 2 | 118 | Indian Territory, | .. | 2 | 9 | 3 | 3 | 17 |
| Texas, | 1 | 2 | 8 | 1 | 2 | 14 | Dakota, | .. | 2 | 5 | 4 | .. | 11 |
| Arkansas, | 1 | 42 | 40 | 78 | 6 | 167 | Arizona, | .. | 1 | 1 | 1 | 1 | 4 |
| Tennessee, | 2 | 82 | 124 | 89 | 1 | 298 | Idaho, | .. | .. | 1 | .. | .. | 1 |
| Kentucky, | 14 | 59 | 30 | 31 | 4 | 138 | | | | | | | |
| Ohio, | .. | .. | 3 | .. | .. | 3 | | 156 | 564 | 627 | 779 | 135 | 2,261 |
| Indiana, | .. | .. | 4 | .. | .. | 4 | | | | | | | |

# BATTLE FIELDS OF THE GREAT C[IVIL WAR]

*Battles are indicated by stars* ★

STATUTE MILES
0    50    100    150    200

MISSOURI

INDEPENDENCE
★ Lexington
LONE JACK ★
★ MARSHALL
★ BOONESBORO
JEFFERSON CITY
Missouri R.
Osage R.
St. LOUIS

ILLINOIS

Wabash R.

INDIAN

LOUISV[ILLE]
LAWRANC[E]
Bu
HARRODSBURG
PERRYV[ILLE]
MUNFO[RD]

• Milford
CARTHAGE ★
★ SPRINGFIELD
RONTON
★ CAIRO
PADUCAH
Ohio R.

★ PEA RIDGE
★ PRAIRIE GROVE
White R.
Arkansas R.

NEW MADRID
PUTNAM'S FERRY ★
ISLAND N.º 10
BELMONT ★
★ COLUMBUS
CLARKSVILLE
★ Ft. DONELSON
Ft. HENRY
Cumberland R.
NASHVILLE ★
HARTS[VILLE]
BOWLING GREEN

KENTU[CKY]

TENNESSEE

FRANKLIN ★
THOMPSON'S STA. ★
★ MURFREESBORO
★ EAGLEVILLE
COLUMBIA
★ SHELBYVILLE
LOOKOUT MT.
★ ATHENS ★ CHICKAMAUGA
ROME ★

ARKANSAS
LITTLE ROCK
★ PINE BLUFF
HELENA
★ Ft. PILLOW
★ JACKSON
★ BRITTON'S LAN[E]
MEMPHIS
★ BOLIVAR
SHILOH OR PITTSBURG LD'G
SALEM ★
★ HERNANDO
HOLLY SPRINGS
★ CORINTH
★ IUKA ★ TUSCUMBIA
★ BRICE'S X RDS. DECATUR
SAVANNAH
CRUMP'S LANDING
Tennessee R.

Ft. HINDMAN ★
★ JENKINS FERRY
Saline R.
Wachita R.

★ COFFEEVILLE
★ RUPELO
★ OKALONA
• Ft. PENBERTON
Black Warrior R.

DAL[TON]
PEACHTR[EE]

ALABAMA

SHREVEPORT ★
CALHOUN ★
★ MILLIKEN'S BEND
★ PLEASANT HILL
SABIN X ROADS ★

★ CANTON
VICKSBURG ★
★ JACKSON
★ CHAMPION HILL
GRAND CULF ★
★ PORT GIBSON
NATCHEZ ★

★ PLANTERSVILLE

MONTGOMERY
Alabama R.
Tombigbee R.

LOUISIANA

Red R.
Sabine R.

ALEXANDRIA ★
MANSURA ★

MISSISSIPPI

Pearl R.

★ PORT HUDSON
GRAND COTEAU ★
★ BATON ROUGE
★ PONCHATOULA
NEW ORLEANS
GEORGIA LANDING ★
★ IRISH BEND
Ft. JACKSON ★ ★ Ft. St. PHILIP
Ft. MORGAN
MOBILE ★
PENSACOLA ★
Ft. PICKENS ★

FL[ORIDA]
Appalachicola R.

GULF   OF   MEXI[CO]

OHIO

PENNSYLVANIA

NEW YORK
TRENTON
PHILADELPHIA
NEW JERSEY
WHEELING
CHAMBERSBURG  CASHTOWN  YORK
GETTYSBURG
HAGERSTOWN  ANTIETAM  BOONSBORO  BALTIMORE
MARTINSBURG  FREDERICK
ROMNEY  WINCHESTER  HARPERS FERRY  ANNAPOLIS  DOVER
GRAFTON
PHILIPPI
CEDAR CR  STRASBURG  WASHINGTON
WEST  CENTRE V  DELAWARE
RICH MOUNTAIN  NEW MARKET  FRONT ROYAL  ALEXANDRIA
VIRGINIA  WARRENTON
CHARLESTON  McDOWELL  HARRISONBURG  CULPEPER  CHANCELLORS
PORT REPUBLIC  WILDERNESS  FREDERICKSBURG
STAUNTON  SPOTSYLVANIA
JAMES R. MECHANICSVILLE  GAINES' MILL
RICHMOND  COLD HARBOR  SEVEN PINES  MALVERN HILL  YORKTOWN
LYNCHBURG  APPOMATTOX C.H.  CITY POINT
PETERSBURG  FT MONROE
FIVE FORKS  NEWPORT NEWS
NORFOLK
DANVILLE
ROANOKE R.  ALBEMARLE S.  ROANOKE ISLAND
BEAN'S STA.
SMOKY MTS  RALEIGH  PLYMOUTH
NORTH CAROLINA  AVERYSBORO  BENTONVILLE
BENTONVILLE  GOLDSBORO  KINSTON
WISE'S FORK  NEUSE  NEW BERN
TRENTON
FAYETTEVILLE
WHITEHALL  CAPE HATTERAS
WILMINGTON
FT FISHER
COLUMBIA  SALUDA R.
SOUTH CAROLINA
AUGUSTA  SANTEE R.
MACON  SALKEHATCHIE  CHARLESTON  FT SUMTER
GEORGIA  BEAUFORT  POCOTALIGO
EDEN  PORT ROYAL  HILTON HEAD
SAVANNAH  FT PULASKI
BRUNSWICK
OLUSTEE  JACKSONVILLE
FLORIDA  ST AUGUSTINE

ATLANTIC OCEAN

CHAMBERSBURG  YORK
CASHTOWN
GETTYSBURG
PENNSYLVANIA
HAGERSTOWN  SOUTH MOUNTAIN
MARTINSBURG  SHARPSBURG  FREDERICK  BALTIMORE
ANTIETAM  MONOCACY
SHEPHERDSTOWN  HARPERS FERRY
SUMMIT POINT  BALLS BLUFF
ROMNEY  WINCHESTER  ANNAPOLIS
KERNSTOWN  POTOMAC R.  DISTRICT OF WASHINGTON  COLUMBIA
CEDAR CR  STRASBURG  MARYLAND
FISHERS HILL  CENTRE V  ALEXANDRIA
FRONT ROYAL  GROVETON  CHESAPEAKE BAY
MANASSAS JUNC  BRISTOE
WARRENTON  RAPPAHANNOCK STA.
NEW MARKET  CULPEPER
HARRISONBURG  WILDERNESS  CHANCELLOR  FREDERICKSBURG
CROSS KEYS  CEDAR MT  OAK GROVE
PORT REPUBLIC  MINE RUN  SPOTSYLVANIA C.H.
STAUNTON  RAPPAHANNOCK R.
VIRGINIA
MECHANICSVILLE  BEAVER DAM CREEK
FAIR OAKS  SEVEN PINES  COLD HARBOR
JAMES R.  RICHMOND  GAINES' MILL  WHITE OAK SWAMP  WILLIAMSBURG
MALVERN HILL  YORK R.  YORKTOWN
APPOMATTOX C.H.  HARRISON'S LANDING  JAMES R.
LYNCHBURG  SAILOR'S CR.  CITY POINT  BIG BETHEL  FT MONROE
FIVE FORKS  PETERSBURG  NEWPORT NEWS
NORFOLK

Statute Miles
0  10  20  30  40  50  60

# RECOMMENDED READING

Civil War in the Making: 1815-1860 — *Avery O. Craven*
The Coming of the Civil War — *Avery O. Craven*
The Irrepressable Conflict — *Arthur C. Cole*

West Point Atlas of American Wars, 2 vols. — *Vincent J. Esposito*
The Story of the Confederacy — *Robert Selph Henry*
Storm Over the Land: A Profile of the Civil War — *Carl Sandburg*
The Confederate States of America — *E. Merton Coulter*
The Compact History of the Civil War — *R. Ernest and Trevor N. Dupuy*
The Civil War and Reconstruction — *James G. Randall*

The Blue and the Gray — *Henry Steele Commager*
The Common Soldier in the Civil War — *Bell Irvin Wiley*
They Fought for the Union — *Francis A. Lord*
Spies for the Blue and Gray — *Harnett Kane*

Battles and Leaders, 4 vols. — *Robert Johnson and Clarence Buel, ed.*
The Civil War at Sea — *Virgil Carrington Jones*
Lee's Lieutenants, 3 vols. — *Douglas Southall Freeman*
R.E. Lee, 4 vols. — *Douglas Southall Freeman*
Mr. Lincoln's Army — *Bruce Catton*
Glory Road — *Bruce Catton*
Stillness at Appomattox — *Bruce Catton*
This Hallowed Ground — *Bruce Catton*
The Generalship of U.S. Grant — *J.F.C. Fuller*
Sherman — Soldier, Realist, American — *B.H. Lidell Hart*
Stonewall Jackson: A Study in Command — *G.F.R. Henderson*
The Civil War: A Soldier's View — *Jay Luvaas, ed.*
As They Saw Forrest — *Robert Selph Henry, ed.*
The Army of the Tennessee — *Stanley Horne*
Lincoln's Plan for Reconstruction — *William B. Hesseltine*
Lincoln's War Cabinet — *Burton J. Hendrick*
Organization and Administration of the Union Army, 2 vols. — *Frederick A. Shannon*
War Department 1861 — *Alfred H. Meneely*
Rebel Brass: The Confederate Command System — *Frank E. Vandiver*
Jefferson Davis — *Hudson Strode*

Photographic History of the Civil War, 10 vols. — *Francis T. Miller and Robert Lanier, ed.*
American Heritage Picture History of the Civil War — *Bruce Catton, ed.*
Divided We Fought — *Hirst Milhollen, Milton Kaplan, Hulen Stuart*
They Who Fought Here — *Bell I. Wiley and Hirst Milhollen*

Notes on U.S. Ordnance, 2 vols. — *James E. Hicks*
U.S. Muskets Rifles, and Carbines — *Arcadi Gluckman*
Firearms of the Confederacy — *Claud Fuller and Richard Stuart*